No More Grains

Quick and Easy Wheat, Grain and Gluten-Free Recipes for Eating Well and Feeling Great!

Sofia Davis

Just to say "Thank you" for purchasing this book, I'd like to give you a gift, absolutely free:

"10 of the Best Paleo Smoothies"

Visit http://seriouspaloeo.com to get access!

Introduction

Being a mom is every woman's dream, and caring for our family's health is our top priority. But taking care of your family is becoming more and more demanding and it involves much more now that it did in the past. The time when moms stayed at home, with their only job to take care of their children, is long gone. Moms nowadays have to work, and balancing work with family and kids is one tough job!

Feeding kids every day is a challenge because they are picky eaters and won't eat just anything you serve up! As if it wasn't enough to provide a healthy diet with all the nutrients they need, some kids can develop allergies or intolerances, such as with wheat or gluten... the list goes on. This means you have to spend more time cooking for them, often having to pay attention to everything little thing they eat. And that can turn into a struggle if you're not well informed and well prepared.

What you need is a repertoire of easy and healthy, gluten-free recipes, and this book is just that, serving you up with 25 delicious and easy to make wheat, grain and gluten-free recipes, which are quick to prepare, even for the busiest moms. You will find a whole range of recipes in this book, both sweet and savory, suitable even for the pickiest of little ones out there!

It's time to stop worrying about your child's food and to start enjoying your time spent together – every minute of it. It's time to invest more in bonding as a family, rather than spending time devising complicated meals. "Quick and Easy" is the solution, even with dietary restrictions. But try not to forget one thing... have fun while cooking! It's not all about the recipe itself, but also about the love you put into the meals you make for your loved ones. Why not try involving your children in the cooking process - show them that delicious food can be quick, easy and fun!

Disclaimer

All rights Reserved. No part of this publication or the information in it may be quoted from or reproduced in any form by means such as printing, scanning, photocopying or otherwise without prior written permission of the copyright holder.

Disclaimer and Terms of Use: Effort has been made to ensure that the information in this book is accurate and complete, however, the author and the publisher do not warrant the accuracy of the information, text and graphics contained within the book due to the rapidly changing nature of science, research, known and unknown facts and internet. The Author and the publisher do not hold any responsibility for errors, omissions or contrary interpretation of the subject matter herein. This book is presented solely for motivational and informational purposes only.

Table of Contents

Breakfast Recipes 7
   Egg and Bacon Cups 8
   Spinach Frittata..9
   Huevos Rancheros - Rustic Scrambled Eggs........11
   Apple and Buckwheat Bread 13
   Coconut Flour and Blueberry Pancakes 15

Main Dishes 17
   Stuffed Bell Peppers 18
   Grilled Salmon with Green Pea Puree..................20
   Bacon Wrapped Chicken 22
   Vegetable Chicken Roulade 24
   Chicken and Mushroom Pizza 26
   Portobello Chicken Burgers 28
   Chicken Strips with Garlic Sauce..........................30
   Roast Chicken and Vegetables 32
   Fish Fingers with Tomato Sauce 34
   Cheesy Zucchini Boats 36

Soups and Salads 38
   Chicken Beet Salad 39
   Cauliflower and Egg Salad 41
   Creamy Pumpkin Soup...43
   Chicken and Vegetable Soup 45
   Coconut and Ginger Chicken Soup 47

Breads and Desserts...49
   Date and Coconut Cookies...................................51
   Cinnamon Swirl Bread 53
   Banana Cake 55
   Chocolate Almond Meal Bread 57

Conclusion 59

Breakfast Recipes

Breakfast is called the most important meal of the day for a reason. Morning meals provide you with the energy needed to start the day, and that is crucial for kids at school who need all the energy they can get to focus properly on their work. For that reason, breakfast needs to be filling and nutritious, loaded with vitamins, minerals and fiber, but also delicious enough to keep them coming back for more.

This chapter consists of 5 of the best gluten, grain and wheat-free recipes, perfect for your children's morning meal. They are all delicious, fragrant and fun recipes and you can even get your kids involved in the cooking process. I guarantee you they'll enjoy what they've made with their own hands even more!

Egg and Bacon Cups

Yes, bacon is gluten-free, wheat-free and grain-free, although it is best to always check the label before buying. This recipe yields some delicious and super simple-to-make savory cups, great to start your day in a filling way.

Prep time: 10 minutes
Cook time: 15 minutes
Servings: 6
Nutritional information: 130 calories/serving

Ingredients:
6 eggs
6 bacon slices
2 tablespoons chopped chives
1 red bell pepper, cored and chopped
Salt, pepper to taste

Directions:
Take a muffin pan and grease it slightly with olive oil. Arrange each bacon slice in muffin cups then crack open the eggs into each cup. Sprinkle with salt and pepper and top with chopped bell pepper and chives. Bake in a preheated oven at 350F for 10-15 minutes or until the eggs are hard. When done, remove from heat and leave to cool down slightly before serving.

Spinach Frittata

Frittata is a dish with Spanish origins, but it's very versatile, and for that reason it's a good choice for your kids' morning meals. This version uses spinach because it's loaded with iron and calcium, but you can replace it with any other fresh vegetable, from bell pepper to asparagus or mushrooms.

Prep time: 10 minutes
Cook time: 15 minutes
Servings: 4
Nutritional information: 300 calories/serving

Ingredients
8 eggs
1 large potato, diced
3 cups baby spinach leaves, shredded
2 tablespoons milk
1/2 teaspoon dried basil
1/2 teaspoon dried oregano
Salt, pepper to taste
4 tablespoons olive oil

Directions:
In a bowl, mix the eggs with the milk, dried basil, oregano, salt and freshly ground pepper. Stir in the spinach and set aside.
Heat the olive oil in a heavy skillet that can go into the oven. Stir in the potato dices and cook for 5-10 minutes, stirring all the time to make sure they cook

evenly. Pour in the egg mixture and lower the heat. Cook the frittata on one side for 5-10 minutes then either flip it over using a platter to make the task easier or simply place the skillet under the broiler for another 5-10 minutes. Serve the frittata warm, with a few fresh vegetables on one side.

Huevos Rancheros - Rustic Scrambled Eggs

Although the name sounds fancy, actually these eggs are very easy to make and the recipe is basic. The final product, however, is flavorful and delicious, perfect to awaken your senses in the morning. The kids will love it because it literally looks like a mess on a plate, and *that* is something they are familiar with!

Prep time: 10 minutes
Cook time: 10 minutes
Servings: 4
Nutritional information: 275 calories/serving

Ingredients:
Scrambled eggs:
2 bacon slices, chopped
8 eggs
1 tomato, peeled, seeded and diced
2 garlic cloves, chopped
1 shallot, finely chopped
2 tablespoons chopped chives
Salt, pepper
2 tablespoons olive oil
Avocado sauce:
1 ripe avocado, peeled
2 tablespoons lemon juice
1 garlic clove
2 tablespoons chopped cilantro
Salt, pepper

Directions:

To make the scrambled eggs, in a bowl, mix the eggs with the chives, salt and pepper and set aside. Heat the olive oil in a heavy skillet then stir in the shallot and garlic. Sauté until soft and translucent then pour in the egg mixture, adding the diced tomato too. Cook the eggs, stirring all the time with a fork or spatula, until the eggs look set. When done, remove from heat and spoon on the serving plates.

To make the avocado sauce, combine the avocado with the lemon juice, garlic clove, cilantro, salt and pepper in a blender and process until well blended and smooth. Drizzle this sauce over the scrambled eggs. Serve immediately.

Apple and Buckwheat Bread

If your kids prefer sweet desserts, this bread is the perfect choice. The apples make it moist and flavorful and, although it's rather a dense bread, it's absolutely delicious next to a cup of tea or glass of warm milk. Make this bread the night before so you can enjoy it in the morning.

Prep time: 10 minutes
Cook time: 40 minutes
Servings: 8
Nutritional information: 155 calories/serving

Ingredients:
1/4 cup flax seeds, ground
1 cup buckwheat flour
1/2 teaspoon gluten-free baking powder
1 pinch of salt
1 teaspoon cinnamon powder
1 egg
1/2 cup milk
2 green apples, peeled and grated
1/4 cup coconut oil
2 tablespoons agave syrup

Directions:
In a bowl, combine the ground flax seeds with the buckwheat flour, baking powder, salt and cinnamon. In another bowl, mix the egg with the milk, coconut oil and agave syrup. Pour this mixture over the flour and

give it a good mix. Fold in the grated apples then transfer the batter into a loaf pan lined with baking paper. Bake in the preheated oven at 350F for 40 minutes. To check for *doneness* insert a toothpick in the center of the bread. If it comes out clean, the bread is done, if it comes out with batter on it, you have to bake it a few more minutes. When done, let it cool in the pan then transfer to a serving platter. Slice and serve!

Coconut Flour and Blueberry Pancakes

Pancakes are a classic for breakfast and there is no way your kids will refuse these. They are easy to make and loaded with flavors that balance together perfectly, creating a delicious and nutritious breakfast for your kids.

Prep time: 10 minutes
Cook time: 20 minutes
Servings: 4
Nutritional information: 285 calories/serving

Ingredients:
1 cup coconut milk
5 eggs
1/2 cup coconut flour
1 teaspoon baking soda
1/2 teaspoon cinnamon powder
2 tablespoons honey
1 cup blueberries, fresh or frozen
1 pinch of salt
2 tablespoons coconut oil

Directions:
In a bowl, combine the coconut milk with the eggs and honey. In another bowl, mix the coconut flour with the baking soda, cinnamon powder and salt. Pour the liquid mixture you made earlier over the flour and give it a good mix. Fold in the blueberries.

Heat a heavy skillet or frying pan over medium flame. Brush the pan with coconut oil then drop a few spoonfuls of batter into the hot pan. Cook on one side for 1-2 minutes until golden brown then flip it over and finish cooking another 1-2 minutes. Repeat until you run out of batter. Serve them fresh, topped with a bit of fresh fruit for a booster of nutrients and vitamins.

Main Dishes

Whilst the kids are growing up they need a whole range of nutrients, from vitamin C for their immune system, to iron and calcium for their bones, not to mention proteins and fat. They are all important for a balanced diet and proper functioning. This chapter includes 10 easy to make recipes for your child's main meal. Make sure to use fresh ingredients and they will love and appreciate your efforts to provide them with a warm and delicious meal every day.

Stuffed Bell Peppers

Bell peppers have a natural sweetness that kids tend to love. Use different colored peppers and fill them with pretty much anything. This recipe is just one option, and a very delicious one at that!

Prep time: 20 minutes
Cook time: 50 minutes
Servings: 6
Nutritional information: 267 calories/serving

Ingredients:
1 pound turkey meat, ground
1 large onion, chopped
2 tablespoons olive oil
1 cup coarse almond meal
1/4 cup chopped dill
1/4 cup chopped parsley
1/2 teaspoon smoked paprika
1/2 cup tomato puree
1 teaspoon dried thyme
1/2 teaspoon dried oregano
Salt, pepper to taste
6 red bell peppers, halved then cored
4 cups water
Juice from 1 lemon

Directions:
Heat the olive oil in a skillet and stir in the onion. Sauté for 5 minutes then add the turkey meat and

almond meal. Remove from heat and stir in the smoked paprika, dried thyme, oregano, chopped dill and parsley, as well as salt and freshly ground pepper to taste. Take each bell pepper and fill it with this mixture. Arrange all the peppers in a large pot with the cut facing up. Mix the water with the lemon juice and a pinch of salt and pour it into the pot, just enough to cover them with liquid, but not to sink them. Cover the pot with a lid and cook the bell peppers for 50 minutes. You can place the pot in the oven too, at 375F for 40-50 minutes. When done, they will be soft and fragrant. Add more lemon juice if you prefer them more tangy. The role of the lemon juice is to balance the flavors. Serve them warm.

Grilled Salmon with Green Pea Puree

It's a good idea to serve your kids a variety of main dishes because this is when they form their eating habits, and the more flavors they try the more their palate will open for new taste experiences. This salmon is tender and the green pea puree will be a hit if you add the right herbs to it.

Prep time: 10 minutes
Cook time: 25 minutes
Servings: 4
Nutritional information: 780 calories/serving

Ingredients:
4 salmon fillets
2 tablespoons lemon juice
1 tablespoon chopped dill
1 tablespoon Dijon mustard
2 cups frozen green peas
2 mint leaves
2 tablespoons coconut oil
1/4 cup coconut milk
Salt, pepper to taste

Directions:
In a bowl, mix the lemon juice with the mustard, chopped dill, salt and freshly ground pepper. Brush each of the four fillets with this mixture. Heat a grill pan over medium flame. Place the fillets in the hot pan, skin facing down. Cook for 3 minutes then flip

them over and finish cooking for 5 more minutes. When done, remove from the pan and set aside.
To make the green pea puree, pour a few cups of water in a pot and bring to a boil with a pinch of salt. Throw in the peas and cook for 10 minutes then drain them. While still hot, transfer the peas in a blender or food processor and pulse until well blended. Stir in the coconut oil, mint leaves and coconut milk, then adjust the taste with salt and pepper.

Serve each fillet over a dollop of green peas puree.

Bacon Wrapped Chicken

I believe every child loves bacon, especially if it's crisp, but you can use this trick to make your kids eat other meats as well. This wrapped chicken is juicy and the bacon flavors goes all the way through, yielding a delicious and fragrant dish.

Prep time: 15 minutes
Cook time: 40 minutes
Servings: 4
Nutritional information: 167 calories/serving

Ingredients:
2 chicken breasts, cut in half lengthwise
8 bacon slices
1 teaspoon dried oregano
2 tablespoons lemon juice
1 garlic clove
Salt, pepper to taste

Directions:
In a bowl, mix the lemon juice with the minced garlic and dried oregano. Add a bit of salt and pepper then brush each piece of chicken with it. Wrap each piece of meat in 2 slices of bacon then arrange them all in a baking pan. Bake in the preheated oven at 350F for 50 minutes. To check if it's done, insert a knife in the meat. If the juices run out clean, the meat is done. If the juices are still pink or red, you have to keep cooking it. When done, remove from oven and let the

meat rest for 10 minutes then serve with your favorite side dish.

Vegetable Chicken Roulade

Although the name sounds fancy, it's actually very easy to make and you can use any vegetables you want. The veggies inside will give it not only flavor, but also moisture.

Prep time: 20 minutes
Cook time: 40 minutes
Servings: 4
Nutritional information: 160 calories/serving

Ingredients:
4 chicken fillets
1 carrot, cut into sticks
1 cup broccoli florets
1/2 teaspoon dried oregano
1/2 teaspoon dried basil
1/2 teaspoon dried rosemary
Salt, pepper to taste
2 tablespoons olive oil

Directions:
Take each chicken fillet and flatten it with a meat tenderizer. Place a few carrot sticks and broccoli florets at the end of each fillet. Sprinkle with the dried herbs, salt and pepper then wrap it like you would with a roll. Secure the ends with a toothpick and arrange the rolls in a baking tray. Drizzle with olive oil and pour 1/4 cup water into the pan. Bake in the preheated oven at 350F for about 1 hour or until golden brown.

When done, let them rest 10 minutes then slice and serve either simple or with some steamed vegetables on one side.

Chicken and Mushroom Pizza

Who doesn't love pizza? Kids sure do and just because they can't eat grains it's not a serious reason to not spoil them with a pizza once in a while. This recipe uses a tapioca flour crust, which is just as delicious as a normal crust, just much healthier and loaded with fibers.

Prep time: 25 minutes
Cook time: 30 minutes
Servings: 8
Nutritional information: 185 calories/serving

Ingredients:
Crust:
1 1/2 cups tapioca flour
2 tablespoons olive oil
1 egg
1/4 cup almond flour
1 teaspoon dried basil
1/2 teaspoon dried oregano
Salt, pepper to taste
Topping:
2 Portobello mushrooms, sliced
1 cooked chicken breast, shredded
1 cup mozzarella cheese, shredded
4 basil leaves, shredded
1/2 cup tomato sauce

Directions:

To make the crust, in a bowl, mix all the ingredients until a smooth paste forms. Line a baking tray with baking paper or a silicone mat and spread the batter into a 1/4-inch thick, round layer. Bake in the preheated oven at 350F for 15 minutes.

Remove the crust from the oven then spread the tomato puree over the crust. Top with the basil leaves, shredded chicken and mozzarella. Bake the pizza for 15 more minutes at 375F then remove from the oven and slice. Serve it warm, while the cheese is still melting.

Portobello Chicken Burgers

Kids love fast-food, but if your child has problems with gluten or wheat, it's best to avoid the ready made burgers which may not only contain gluten, but also have no nutrients at all due to being over-processed, rich in fat and with unhealthy additives. Homemade burgers are delicious and you can customize them any way you want by adding or removing ingredients. This recipe uses mushrooms instead of burger buns, which makes them even more nutritious.

Prep time: 20 minutes
Cook time: 20 minutes
Servings: 5
Nutritional information: 188 calories/serving

Ingredients:
10 Portobello mushrooms
1 pound chicken meat, ground
1 carrot, grated
1/4 cup chopped dill
2 green onions, chopped
2 garlic cloves, minced
2 tablespoons chopped cilantro
1 tomato, sliced
5 lettuce leaves
Salt, pepper to taste

Directions:

To make the chicken burgers, mix the ground meat with the grated carrot, dill, garlic, cilantro and green onions, then adjust the taste with a pinch of salt and freshly ground pepper. Mix well until it comes together like a dough. Wet your hands and form small burgers. Set them aside. Try to make 5 burgers from these quantities, although you can make more or less, depending on how thick you want them to be.

To cook the burgers, heat a grill pan over medium flame. When the pan is hot, place the burgers for 5-7 minutes on both sides. When done, remove them in a plate and set aside.

Now you have to cook the mushrooms too. Place them on the same grill, sprinkle them with salt and cook on both sides until juicy and cooked all the way through.

To serve the burgers, place them between two Portobello mushrooms, top with a slice of tomato and a lettuce leaf and serve them fresh.

Chicken Strips with Garlic Sauce

If there's one thing you get to learn about kids and their eating habits, it's how much they love finger food! And these chicken strips are perfect to grab and chew on when you're feeling hungry. The mustard sauce is a delight because its taste is only mild and flavorful and the whole dish is rich in proteins and fibers.

Prep time: 20 minutes
Cook time: 25 minutes
Servings: 6
Nutritional information: 300 calories/serving

Ingredients:
Chicken strips:
2 chicken breast, cut into thin strips
2 eggs
1/2 cup almond meal
1/2 cup shredded coconut
1 teaspoon Italian seasoning
Salt, pepper
1 cup coconut oil for frying
Sauce:
1/4 cup sour cream
2 garlic cloves, minced
2 tablespoons chopped dill
1 pinch of salt
1 tablespoon lemon juice

Directions:

To make the chicken strips, in a bowl mix the almond meal with the shredded coconut, salt, pepper and Italian seasoning. In another bowl, beat the eggs. Heat the coconut oil in a large frying pan. Take each meat strip and dip it first in egg then roll it in the almond meal mixture. Drop it into the hot oil and cook it until golden brown, about 3-4 minutes. Remove it on paper towels and repeat with the remaining meat.

To make the sauce, combine all ingredients in a serving bowl.

To serve the chicken, arrange them on a plate and put the sauce bowl in the middle. Dip each strip into sauce when eating.

Roast Chicken and Vegetables

Probably the easiest way of cooking chicken is to roast it. But this is also the technique that gives it the most flavor, and adding a few vegetables only enhances the taste and makes it a complete meal, great for any day of the week.

Prep time: 10 minutes
Cook time: 1 hour
Servings: 8
Nutritional information: 220 calories/serving

Ingredients:
1 whole chicken, cut into smaller pieces
1 pound broccoli, cut into small florets
2 large carrots, finely sliced
1/2 pound mushrooms, washed and cut in wedges
1 red onion, sliced
4 garlic cloves, crushed
2 tablespoons lemon juice
2 tablespoons olive oil
1 teaspoon smoked paprika
1 teaspoon dried rosemary
1 tablespoon lemon zest

Directions:
In a bowl, mix the lemon juice with the olive oil, paprika, rosemary and lemon zest, as well as salt and freshly ground pepper. Brush each piece of meat with

this mixture. The lemon juices and spices will infuse the meat perfectly.

Arrange all the vegetables in a pan and top them with the meat pieces. Bake in the preheated oven at 375F for 1 hour or until the meat is cooked through and golden brown. To check if it's done, insert a knife in the meat. If the juices run out clean, it is done. If the juices are still pink, cook it a bit more.

When done, remove it from the oven and serve immediately, while warm.

Fish Fingers with Tomato Sauce

There's no need to buy fish fingers from the supermarket when you don't even know what ingredients they use. You can make them at home and serve them with a flavorful, delicious tomato sauce.

Prep time: 15 minutes
Cook time: 20 minutes
Servings: 4
Nutritional information: 397 calories/serving

Ingredients:
Fish fingers:
4 white fish fillets (such as cod, halibut or tilapia)
1 cup almond meal
1 teaspoon lemon zest
2 eggs
Salt, pepper
1/2 cup coconut oil for frying
Tomato sauce:
1/2 cup tomato puree
1 teaspoon dried basil
1 pinch cayenne pepper
1 garlic clove, minced
1 pinch dried thyme

Directions:
To make the fish fingers, cut the fish fillets into strips and season them with salt and pepper.

In a bowl, combine the almond meal with the lemon zest. In another bowl, beat the eggs.
Heat the coconut oil in a frying pan or skillet. Take each piece of fish and dip it into egg then roll it into the almond mixture. Drop it into the hot oil and cook 2-3 minutes until golden brown on both sides. Repeat with all the fish pieces, but don't bulk them all at once in the pan. They have to remain crisp so cook them gradually.

To make the sauce, mix all the ingredients together in a bowl. Serve the fish fingers with dipping sauce.

Cheesy Zucchini Boats

Zucchini are a good source of vitamins and their very mild taste makes them perfect for kids dishes. Cutting them to resemble a boat and stuffing them with a delicious mixture makes them much more appealing to kids.

Prep time: 25 minutes
Cook time: 30 minutes
Servings: 6
Nutritional information: 135 calories/serving

Ingredients:
3 young zucchinis, cut in half lengthwise
1/2 pound chicken meat, ground
2 tablespoons chopped parsley
2 garlic cloves, minced
1 green onion, chopped
1 red bell pepper, cored and chopped
1 cup mozzarella cheese, shredded
Salt, pepper

Directions:
Take each zucchini half and, using a teaspoon, scoop out the flesh, leaving the skins intact. Chop the flesh and place it into a bowl. Add the ground chicken, chopped parsley, garlic, green onion and bell pepper and mix well. Season with salt and pepper then spoon this mixture back into each zucchini boat. Top with a bit of cheese and place them all in a baking tray. Bake

in the preheated oven at 350F for 30 minutes or until soft and golden brown on top. When done, let them cool slightly and serve them with sour cream.

Soups and Salads

Soups and fresh salads are just as important in a child's diet as main dishes or snacks, and as much as kids will kick up a fuss about eating their greens, you have to keep trying. The flavors are completely different and there are definitely more nutrients in a fresh salad than in fried chicken. This chapter includes five delicious soup and salad recipes tailored for your kids, although grown-ups will love their richness and flavors too!

Chicken Beet Salad

This is probably the most basic salad recipe, but it's very filling and nutritious. Vegetables and chicken come together to create a complete dish that can easily be your kids' lunch or dinner. This version of the recipes uses lettuce, but you can replace it with spinach, arugula or even kale if your kids like them.

Prep time: 15 minutes
Cook time: 5 minutes
Servings: 4
Nutritional information: 120 calories/serving

Ingredients:
1 chicken breast, sliced
1 head lettuce, shredded
1 cooked small beet, cubed
1/4 cup dried cranberries
Juice from 1/2 lemon
2 tablespoons balsamic vinegar
1 tablespoon chopped parsley
1 pinch cumin powder
2 tablespoons olive oil
Salt, pepper

Directions:
In a bowl, whisk the lemon juice with the balsamic vinegar, chopped parsley, cumin powder and olive oil, as well as salt and freshly ground pepper. Set aside.

Arrange the lettuce on a platter. Top it with the cooked beet and cranberries. Add the chicken slices too then drizzle everything with the lemon juice dressing you made earlier. Serve the salad fresh.

Cauliflower and Egg Salad

This is not a common kind of salad because it doesn't have green vegetables like most salads do. Instead, it's a richer and creamier cauliflower salad, also loaded with protein and calcium. The cauliflower can easily be replaced with potatoes for a more filling version.

Prep time: 15 minutes
Cook time: 25 minutes
Servings: 4
Nutritional information: 146 calories/serving

Ingredients:
1 head cauliflower, cut into small florets
2 eggs, hard boiled
4 tablespoons olive oil
1 tablespoon chopped parsley
1 red onion, sliced
1/2 cup black olives
juice from 1/2 lemon
Salt, pepper

Directions:
Place the cauliflower in a steamer and cook it until tender. Transfer it into a bowl when done.
Peel off the shell of the eggs and remove the hard egg yolks. Chop the egg white into the bowl over the cauliflower. Add into the bowl, followed by the red onion and chopped parsley. Mix the egg yolks with the

olive oil and lemon juice. Add salt and pepper to taste and spoon this mixture over the vegetables. Mix gently with a spoon and serve the salad fresh. If you replace the cauliflower with potatoes, try boiling them instead of steaming to make sure they preserve enough moisture.

Creamy Pumpkin Soup

This soup is included here for its rich color that kids will love. The more colorful the food, the better! Plus, its taste is different, and if your kids like new flavor experiences this food will definitely be a hit. Even if they are picky eaters, it's still worth a try, although you can replace the pumpkin with potatoes or sweet potatoes and even carrots. Other vegetables can turn into creamy soups too, such as broccoli, cauliflower or roasted bell peppers.

Prep time: 15 minutes
Cook time: 30 minutes
Servings: 4
Nutritional information: 115 calories/serving

Ingredients:
4 cups pumpkin cubes
2 bacon slices
1 shallot, chopped
2 garlic cloves, chopped
2 tablespoons pumpkin seeds
4 cups water or homemade stock
Salt, pepper to taste

Directions:
Heat a soup pot and cook the bacon slices. Remove them and add the shallot and garlic in the remaining fat. Cook for 5 minutes until soft and translucent then add the pumpkin cubes and stock. Season with salt

and pepper and cook for 30 minutes until tender. Puree the soup with an immersion blender then pour in serving bowl. To serve, crush the crisp bacon slices and sprinkle them over the soup then top with a few pumpkin seeds for even more texture and nutrients. Serve it right away.

Chicken and Vegetable Soup

The most basic of soups is the chicken and veggie one, but it is also the most comforting one and why not make it for your kids considering it's so easy and quick to make. Especially in the cold season, this soup is a real treat.

Prep time: 10 minutes
Cook time: 50 minutes
Servings: 8
Nutritional information: 114 calories/serving

Ingredients:
1 whole chicken, cut into smaller pieces
2 large carrots, cut into thick sticks
1 celery stalk, sliced
1 onion, left whole
1 green bell pepper, cored and diced
1 red bell pepper, cored and sliced
1 small zucchini, diced
1 bay leaf
2 tablespoons chopped parsley
Salt, pepper
8 cups water

Directions:
Place the chicken in a pot and cover it with water. Add a pinch of salt and cook it for 20 minutes. Stir in the rest of the vegetables and the bay leaf and keep cooking for 30 minutes more. Remove the meat from

the pot and shred it off the bone. Remove the bay leaf and the whole onion then transfer the shredded meat back into the pot. Serve the soup hot or warm, in a large serving bowl, topped with chopped parsley. It's absolutely delicious with all those flavors balancing each other out.

Coconut and Ginger Chicken Soup

If you or your kids prefer richer soups, this coconut and chicken broth is definitely what you want. The flavors are different from any other soup you've had, but the final result is comforting and delicious. Plus, the ginger is a great immune system booster.

Prep time: 10 minutes
Cook time: 30 minutes
Servings: 6
Nutritional information: 135 calories/serving

Ingredients:
1 chicken breast, cubed
1 teaspoon grated ginger
1 cup coconut milk
3 cups water or homemade chicken stock
1 cup mushrooms, sliced
1 carrot, diced
1 celery stalk, diced
2 tablespoons chopped cilantro
juice from 1 lime
Salt, pepper

Directions:
Combine the water with the ginger in a soup pot. Stir in salt and pepper then add the chicken meat and cook for 10 minutes. Add the mushrooms, carrot and celery stalk and cook for another 20 minutes on low heat, allowing the flavors to combine. Stir in the

coconut milk and lime juice then remove from heat. Pour in a large serving bowl and top with chopped cilantro to serve.

Breads and Desserts

No meal is complete without dessert, but things get complicated when it comes to children. It is best to avoid overly sweet desserts and instead try to give them something healthy and nutritious. This is what this chapter is all about. These breads and desserts are easy to make, but are loaded with nutrients for your kids. You will find in this chapter five recipes that can be made ahead of time, easily stored for later, but best of all, loaded with fibers and minerals - great for your growing children!

Baked Apples and Pears

Fruits are a great choice for your children's desserts, but keep in mind that you can create various delicious and healthy versions with just a few ingredients. Spoil your kids with this and they will love you for it!

Prep time: 10 minutes
Cook time: 30 minutes
Servings: 4
Nutritional information: 400 calories/serving

Ingredients:
4 apples
4 pears
2 tablespoons honey
juice from 1/2 lemon
1/2 cup almonds, coarsely chopped
1/2 cup raisins

Directions:
In a bowl, combine the almonds, raisins, honey and lemon juice. Take each apple and pear and carefully scoop out the core. Fill each fruit with the almond and raisins mixture and arrange all the fruits in a baking tray. Bake in the preheated oven at 350F for 20-30 minutes or until tender and fragrant. Serve them warm or cold - they're just as tasty!

Date and Coconut Cookies

Don't forget that desserts don't have to be loaded with sugar. Instead, make sure your kids get healthy sweets made with ingredients they love. These cookies are a perfect example of a dessert rich in fibers and calcium, delicious and fragrant.

Prep time: 10 minutes
Cook time; 20 minutes
Servings: 8
Nutritional information: 209 calories/serving

Ingredients:
1/4 cup coconut flour
1/4 cup almond butter
1/4 cup applesauce
1 cup dates, pitted
1/2 cup shredded coconut
2 eggs
1 pinch cinnamon powder
1 pinch salt
1 teaspoon vanilla extract
1/2 cup raisins
1/2 cup walnuts, chopped

Directions:
Combine the almond butter and dates in a food processor and pulse until well blended. Add the applesauce and coconut flour and process until it comes together. Stir in the eggs, shredded coconut,

cinnamon, salt and vanilla extract and pulse to mix well. Fold in the raisins and walnuts. Line a baking tray with baking paper. Using an ice cream scoop, drop spoonfuls of batter onto the baking tray. The reason we are using a scoop is to make sure the cookies are even, but a normal spoon works too. Bake the cookies in the preheated oven at 375F for 20-25 minutes or until golden brown and fragrant. When done, let them cool in the pan then transfer into an airtight container to store for up to one week. Storing them like this means they will preserve the taste and moisture for a longer period of time.

Cinnamon Swirl Bread

This is a bread that tastes like dessert. If you toast it in the morning it can be a delicious breakfast, if you eat it plain it can be a good afternoon snack, but if you eat it topped with coconut cream it turns into a lovely, gooey dessert. Versatile recipes are great for busy moms!

Prep time: 10 minutes
Cook time: 40 minutes
Servings: 14
Nutritional information: 176 calories/serving

Ingredients:
1 cup almond meal
1/2 cup walnuts, ground
1/4 cup coconut flour
1/4 cup flax seeds, ground
1 teaspoon baking soda
1 teaspoon baking powder
6 eggs
1/4 cup almond milk
1/2 cup coconut oil
1/4 cup honey
2 teaspoons cinnamon
1 tablespoon cocoa powder
1 teaspoon vanilla extract
1 pinch of salt

Directions:

In a bowl, combine the almond meal with the ground walnuts, coconut flour, ground flax seeds, salt, baking soda and baking powder. In another bowl, combine the eggs with the almond milk, coconut oil, honey and vanilla extract. Pour this mixture over the flour and give it a good mix, making sure the dry ingredients are well incorporated. Remove 1/3 of the batter into a bowl and stir in the cinnamon and cocoa powder.

Line a loaf pan with baking paper. Pour half of the vanilla, simple batter into the pan. Top with the cinnamon batter then spoon in the remaining vanilla batter. Take a toothpick and dip it into the batter, bringing the cinnamon layer up to the surface to create a marbling effect. Bake the loaf in the preheated oven at 350F for 40 minutes. To check for *doneness*, insert a toothpick into the center of the loaf. It's done when the toothpick comes out clean. If it still has batter traces, keep baking a few more minutes then check again.

When done, remove the pan from the oven and let the loaf cool in the pan then transfer to a wire rack or serving platter. Slice and serve.

Banana Cake

Fragrant and rich, this cake is a real delight, but also a versatile recipe. If you add cocoa powder or chopped chocolate, it turns into a different recipe with different flavors. Either way, it's a moist and healthy cake, safe for your kids to indulge on for their sweeter moments!

Prep time: 15 minutes
Cook time: 40 minutes
Servings: 10
Nutritional information: 280 calories/serving

Ingredients:
1 1/2 cups almond butter
3 bananas, mashed
4 eggs
1/4 cup honey
1 teaspoon apple cider vinegar
1 teaspoon cinnamon powder
1 teaspoon baking soda
1/2 teaspoon baking powder
1/2 cup coconut flour
1 pinch of salt

Directions:
In a bowl, mix the almond butter with the honey, then stir in the eggs one by one. Add the mashed bananas and the vinegar. Take another bowl and mix the coconut flour with the baking soda, baking powder, salt and cinnamon. Incorporate this dry mixture into

the butter and mix well with a spatula until the batter looks smooth. Pour the batter into a 9-inch cake pan lined with baking paper. Bake in a preheated oven at 350F for 40 minutes or until fragrant and golden brown. To make sure it's baked, insert a toothpick in the center of the cake. If it comes out clean, the cake is done, but if it still has cake batter traces, bake it for a few more minutes. When done, remove from the oven and let it cool to room temperature before slicing.

Chocolate Almond Meal Bread

This recipe yields a delicious, fragrant bread which can be improved with the addition of dried fruits or fresh berries. The bread itself is moist, airy and has an intense chocolate flavor.

Prep time: 10 minutes
Cook time: 40 minutes
Servings: 8
Nutritional information: 163 calories/serving

Ingredients:
2 cups almond meal
1/4 cup flax seeds, ground
1/4 cup cocoa powder
1 teaspoon baking soda
1 pinch of salt
4 eggs
2 tablespoons honey
2 tablespoons coconut oil
1 teaspoon apple cinder vinegar

Directions:
In a bowl, combine the almond meal with the ground flax seeds, cocoa powder, baking soda and salt. In another bowl, mix the eggs with the honey until light in color then add the coconut oil and vinegar. Gradually stir in the flour mixture and mix until smooth. Spoon this batter into a loaf pan lined with baking paper and bake in the preheated oven at 350F for 30-40 minutes

or until a toothpick inserted in the center of the loaf comes out clean. When done, remove from the oven and let it cool in the pan before serving.

Conclusion

As busy as you are, there is nothing more important than your child's health and it concerns you more than anything else. Considering that we are being bombarded with products loaded with additives and other chemicals, it's very hard to find quality grain, wheat and gluten-free products that are ready to eat. The only solution is to cook at home for your kids, with fresh ingredients, so you can be confident about everything that they're eating. After all, intolerances to certain food can turn into serious health problems further down the line if not controlled.

The recipes found in this book are very versatile. Feel free to play with ingredients and customize them according to your child's liking. Don't forget that another huge time-saving trick is to make larger quantities and freeze for later. This way, when you come home from work, tired and not even wanting to see the inside of a kitchen, you can just reheat a delicious meal in seconds. Dinner's ready.

Most of all, these quick and easy recipes free you up to enjoy those precious moments spent with your kids. Make them feel you are doing everything you can to relief their allergies, if they have them, and let them know they can have a completely normal life by choosing the right foods. This is one of the hardest parts of a mom's job, and you've made a great start just by reading this far!

Enjoy this book?

A lot of love went into making this book! I'd be so grateful if you could take the time to leave an honest review and let me know what you liked about it.

https://www.amazon.com/gp/css/order-history *and click on Digital Orders.*

Made in the USA
Lexington, KY
09 April 2015